Raven's Light

A Tale of Alaska's White Raven

Marianne Schlegelmilch

Raven's light

A Tale of Alaska's White Raven

Marianne Schlegelmilch

Foreword by
Chris Kiana

Publication Consultants
since 1978

PO Box 221974 Anchorage, Alaska 99522-1974
books@publicationconsultants.com
www.publicationconsultants.com

ISBN 978-1-59433-067-4

Library of Congress Catalog Card Number: 2008923190

Copyright 2008 by Marianne Schlegelmilch
—First Edition—

This is a work of fiction. All of the characters, organizations, and events portrayed in this novel are either products of the author's imagination or are used fictitiously.

Manufactured in the United States of America

To
Bill and his brothers
And
To the enduring power of our inner light

Contents

A Tribute

The Alaska legend of the white raven is a message of hope. In her book, Marianne Schlegelmilch has done an excellent job of weaving together this legend of hope with the very real hope of military veterans suffering from PTSD (post-traumatic stress disorder) that they will be able to find a way to heal from the trauma of war and become whole once again. Veterans I know who have read advance copies of *Raven's Light* not only enjoyed it, but found it struck a strong emotional chord deep inside them. My congratulations and sincere thanks to Ms. Schlegelmilch for having written this book. It's a book of good heart. *Bill K.*

Acknowledgements

Editing
Rebecca Goodrich
Homer, Alaska
Joyce Baker Porte
Homer, Alaska

Cover Art
Fred-Christian Freer
At Full Spectrum Studio
Fairbanks, Alaska

Inspiration
Alaska and its People
Alaska Men of Valor:
Lloyd, Jim K, Bill K, Bill S,
and all who served with honor

Encouragement, support, and Patient Guidance
Ann, Joyce, Winnie, Ron, Henry,
Evan, and most of all, Bill

Foreword
by Chris Kiana

At first reading, one might think that this book is written only about ravens, but not so. In reading this book, the reader soon discovers a series of stories and events that weave the lives of ravens and humans together. Each chapter in this short but intricately written book, reveals its own sequence of unique events. Woven together with the other chapters as the story unfolds, each episode evokes images of the struggles and occurrences of real life, taking the reader on an interesting and compelling journey through the full gamut of human emotion.

Intense in symbolism, this realistic portrayal of the struggle between peace and harmony in the face of drama and destruction, will evoke in the reader a sense that he has read a much longer piece of work.

Skillfully woven together, these individual episodes in the lives of both humans and ravens come together to bring a message of peace and hope to those who take the time to absorb the book's message. The message of *Raven's Light* will bring to readers of diverse experience and backgrounds, a glimpse into the triumph of good over evil, hope over despair and light over darkness. Seemingly simplistic in the story's evolution of the search for inner peace, *Raven's Light* is a book filled with deep insights and carefully woven truths, written by an author who truly understands the human struggle.

Ever since man first put pen to paper and probably even before, the use of symbolism in writing has been used to weave stories that are both entertaining and meaningful...*Raven's Light* is such a story.

Relax as you read and let the author take you into her world of symbolistic reality in this story that will entertain you and fill you with the hopeful discovery of inner peace.

Prologue
Raven–creator, trickster, bringer of
storms, and portent of awareness.

Ravens have long provided for an abundance of legends in Alaska. These stories, where truth meets fiction, reflect the simple beauty of a great land and its unique people. The 2002 sighting of a white raven in Fairbanks, Alaska inspires this story, as do the people who live throughout this place called the Last Frontier. This tale, wound both around numerous sightings of a white raven and the good people of Alaska, is set in the Matanuska Valley well to the south of the area where the white raven first sprang from the shadows of Denali. There, among the magnificent mountains, sprawling glaciers and vast expanses of valley terrain, unfold these fictional stories about fictional characters; many named in honor of real Alaskans I hold dear. Emerging within these stories, is the main character, a raven named Zak. Zak represents all of us who have ever been forced by life's events to retreat into the gray world of faded hope and trampled dreams. His story tells how the inner light that shines within us all begins to glow in his heart again.

Marianne Schlegelmilch

One Valley Raven

A few villagers in the shadows of the mountain called Denali were the first to see the white raven early in the fall, right about the time the days and nights were of equal length. During the autumnal equinox magpies are no longer seen in great numbers, and the ravens seem to sprout, like an abundance of black-feathered dots, in most clearings in Interior and South Central Alaska.

At first, no one mentioned the strange sighting of the white raven, with most people thinking their eyes had played tricks on them. Eventually, one person said something to another person, and the legend was born – even making its way into the big city newspaper in Anchorage.

Aside from a passing curiosity, most people gave little notice to the unusual sighting other than to wonder where the ravens had been all summer, and how interesting it was that one returned in the color of white.

The October Alaska day was crisp and cool with the warmth of the sun in stark contrast to both the icy blue sky, and the ambient temperature. By mid-morning, a dense, gray fog had begun to roll in off Cook Inlet. Winding around the mountains, it slithered along the sides of each peak in wispy white fingers, a portent of the coming wind. Sliding into every crack and fissure of the steep cliffs, it anchored itself to the mountains before slowly extending a blanket of gray across the floor of the Matanuska Valley.

When the fog lifted, the ravens, not seen by anyone since last spring, were the first to appear. From the rolled down window of the old station wagon he had driven since leaving his job as historian for a large museum, Wils Kelderman quietly watched the arriving birds. Now in his mid sixties, he was free to pursue his doctorate in ornithology full time, an endeavor that had long taken a back seat to his need for an occupation that would actually generate income. Raising his binoculars to get a closer look, he studied the activities of the ravens. The behaviors of these gregarious birds would be the focus of his doctoral thesis.

The raven chatter was more active than usual among the gathering birds as they fluttered and tussled for the best location on the ground. The flap continued for some time, until all had settled into their comfort zone. That is, except for the few who claimed to have seen the white raven. They stayed off to themselves and were silent.

One raven, named Zak, was the focus of Wils current attention. Larger than most of the other ravens who inhabited the area, Zak had an interesting tweak of feathers under his chin that persistently stuck outward, making him easy to identify. Wils, having spotted this interesting feature, pulled his voice recorder out of his shirt pocket and noted this very fact before rolling up his window and driving away.

Zak paid little attention either to the white raven situation or to the cacophonous flurry around him. Preferring to avoid the clamoring birds, he flew to the top of a light pole. The pole stood in the parking lot of an office building in Wasilla, about a block away from where the others had gathered. Hopping along the edge of the square metal box that housed the light, he fluffed his feathers, before setting down the bag of French fries he had just pilfered on the way over from the nearby hamburger stand. Alone as usual, he ate his lunch.

Pondering the mountains to the east and the others to the west as he sat eating, he steeled himself against the afternoon breeze that ruffled his feathers and threatened to knock him off balance. Pushing his talons hard against the cold metal of the light box, he steadied himself, ignoring the calls of several passing ravens to gather with them in the parking lot nearby. When he felt securely braced against the wind, he tucked his head underneath his wing, closed his eyes, and slept.

In a couple of hours, he would awaken, nibble on the remnants of the fries and head for the mountain ash trees in a nearby neighborhood. There he would sit with others like himself, eating the red berries from the trees until he was tired again and unable to remember what he was trying to forget. This was his routine. It never varied day after day after day. It had been this way since the day that so long ago had changed his life forever.

While other ravens came and went across the Valley, Zak slept. Cars in the parking lot below moved in and out, belching thick clouds of gray smoke in their exhaust as their owners jockeyed them in and out of the narrow spaces. Oblivious to it all, Zak hung onto the pole as he napped, until a whomp on the side of it jolted him awake. Instantly he was alert. The metal vibrated, whipping the pole back and forth from the force of the blow, threatening to bounce him over the edge and to the ground. Standing on the ground below was an irate, sinewy man holding a metal shovel as if it were a baseball bat.

"I oughtta bring my twenty-two. That'll get riduv im," Ed sputtered, his words shooting through the air in the direction of his wife, Lucy.

"Somebody oughtta do something," she agreed, continuing to sweep the area clean of fallen fries and pieces of the cardboard container that once held them.

The elderly caretaker of the building was growing tired of cleaning up after the ever-present Zak. Nothing he had tried seemed to rid the area of the bird and the mess he brought with him each day. Lucy was equally tired of seeing her husband upset by the squatter who had taken up residence on the light pole. Hardworking and diligent in keeping the area one of the cleanest in Wasilla, they had little tolerance for policing a pesky bird who, as far as they were concerned, could just as well find a light pole somewhere other than over the parking lot that they had been hired to care for.

"Take that, old man," Zak croaked, cocking his head and zinging a couple of fries down Ed's way with the sweep of one wing.

Wils Kelderman watched the scene unfold as he turned out of the parking lot and waited at the stoplight for traffic to clear. For a moment, he wished he could have been like this bird and able to so easily unload his annoyances at people, like those who had made his days at the museum an endless blur of tedious inertia. Maybe then he might not have developed the heart condition that forced his early retirement.

Shivering a ripple down his body to re-settle his feathers, Zak lifted his feet one at a time and turned sideways on the light box. That felt better. Now that he was awake, he might as well fly over to the berry trees and leave Ed to sputter about a couple of fries on the ground.

"Are those fries the most important thing you have to worry about in life?" The words spewed from his open beak as he flew off.

Ever since the big oil spill, Zak had little concern for the world around him and even less tolerance for those who did. How could they worry about silly gatherings and fries on the ground and such when thousands of his kind had their lives cut suddenly short, smothered by the thick, tacky, slow death of crude oil destroying the ability of their feathers to hold heat and seeping its poison through their skin.

Zak didn't know why he had been spared and the others had not. They had all been there together on that terrible day, doing what birds do to savor the abundant riches of the sea. He didn't even know why he had been near the beaches when the oil spill occurred. It was not his usual haunt. Seldom did larger ravens, like him, gather along the ocean, an area more frequented by their cousins, the crows. That day, though, he had been there with the other birds, soaring above the waves, dipping his wings in the sea foam that brushed the beaches and otherwise reveling in the life-sustaining qualities of the sea. That day he had flown back to his valley relaxed and refreshed, totally invigorated, and aglow with renewed appreciation for the bounty of the earth.

Only hours later, the disaster struck. Like so many, he learned of it by word of mouth. Later it would be determined that eleven million gallons of crude oil had spilled into the pristine waters off the coast of Alaska. Like so many others, he flocked at once to the beaches. When he got there, he saw the devastation. Helplessly, he watched as people thronged to the area. Frantically they tried to clean the oil from the feathers of the endless mass of birds and sea mammals who lay glued to the earth by the thick black, tacky mess. The clean-up task was monumental and one that proved to be futile as well. For weeks, it went on, then into months, as people gathered to try to help the birds and the otters, and even whales whom the oil had engulfed.

Zak tried to bring food to some of the birds, but they couldn't eat. They were unable to force their beaks open against the gooey crude oil that shrouded them alive in the rubbery casket that the beach had become. Held down by the weight of the oil and weakened from the cold, they couldn't even right themselves to swallow.

Desperate to help save them a shivering, frozen death from the loss of insulation from their feathers, Zak tried to shelter them with his outstretched wings, but his wings were too small to make any impact on the hundreds of miles of spoiled beaches that held hundreds of thousands of doomed birds. He tried to get others to join him wing to wing to form a makeshift shelter, but all were too busy helping the overwhelming numbers of wounded, and tending to what had become the dying fields.

Zak watched, overwhelmed and helpless to respond. For days on end, he struggled to find a way to save the birds. Every so often, he flew inland for miles, trying to escape the sickening view that even distance would not separate from his mind. Once he tried carrying several birds, one by one, into nearby lakes in an attempt to rinse them off. Picking up leaves and twigs in his beak, he used them to try to scrape the tar off the birds, but nothing penetrated the thick gooey mess that matted the birds' feathers to their bodies. Besides, the movement alone was too much for many of them.

When he could no longer watch them die, he flew away, never to return again. It was then he discovered the berry tree and ate the fruit that made him laugh again, at least for a while. Half a million birds and countless other creatures died that day, and in the days after the great oil spill. In spite of all the years that had gone by, and in spite of his own advancing age, time had done nothing to lessen the image of those beaches in Zak's mind.

Chapter Two
Holiday Shoppers

October gave way to November, as the days grew rapidly shorter in the fading light of the arctic winter. The icy air of night left the Valley covered with frost most mornings. The sun, thirsty, melted it and drank it from the earth by afternoon. When night fell again, the cycle repeated until with the shrinking days, the sun could no longer keep up with the increasing frost. Stiff winds had taken what was left of the leaves from the trees. The land, empty of color, yawned a brown sigh as it settled into winter's bosom. Bundled gently with each new snow, it rested.

By now, the ravens were a common sight. Aside from the occasional eagle, they were the only birds seen on a regular basis. Like black lumps of coal scattered over the fresh dustings of snow that came and went over the first weeks of fall, they gave contrast to the grayness of the days and brought life to the slumbering earth. Going about their daily routine, they often linked their activities to those of humans.

Amusing to some and annoying to others, the ravens' antics were an ever-present diversion in the otherwise quiet of winter. No matter which way you saw them, one thing on which all could agree, was that the coal-colored gregarious birds knew how to attract attention.

———

The Wednesday before Thanksgiving began as an unseasonably warm, sunny day. The parking lots of the grocery stores in the Matanuska Valley were, as most throughout the state, crowded with all shapes and sizes of vehicles. At least half of these were pick-up trucks. All were covered in the brown, sloshy grime that the cold misty drizzle of emerging winter had left for vehicles' tires to kick up as they moved along the roads. Stores were quickly selling out of windshield washer solution as shoppers bought up existing stocks. Drivers could be seen all over parking lots throughout the area, carrying the gallon bottles out to their vehicles, and lifting their hoods to refill the blue fluid. Many would also take this opportunity to change their old worn wiper blades for new ones to help them see better on the dark, dirty roads. During this time of year, area dumpsters were filled with more than the usual amount of the empty bottles and cardboard packaging from these items, and fewer of the remnants of fast food take-out that the ravens loved to indulge in.

Crowds of people came from the far reaches of the enormous twenty-three thousand square-mile Mat-Su Valley to gather inside the stores. Mingling in the tightly packed aisles, they searched for the special items that would help them make their

Thanksgiving Day a true feast. On days such as this, right before a holiday, it was not uncommon for last minute shoppers to find that the store shelves were half-empty of flour, brown sugar, frozen turkeys, and other essential items. Most who had lived in Alaska for any length of time knew that if they wanted their Thanksgiving to be special, they needed to shop ahead to avoid these seasonal shortages. In spite of the scarcity of many items in the stores, though, people remained cordial, often laughing at their own lack of foresight. In true Alaskan spirit, they made the holiday shopping experience its own type of special celebration.

Attracted by the wave of shoppers moving into and out of the stores, ravens, known to be opportunistic, also gathered in large numbers around the parking lots. Looking for special treats among the scores of open bed pick-ups that held groceries destined for homes far and wide, they gathered over the parking lots to take advantage of the greater selection of goods during this special season.

One plump raven named Myra was particularly excited about an old blue pick-up that was parked off to the side of the lot and away from the others. At first she circled over it several times before finally swooping past the faded blue beater, her reflection flashing in the glass among the decals and bumper stickers splattered over the windows. She was elated to see the bed of the old truck packed with fresh bags of dog food and boxes of neatly stacked canned goods, vegetables, and best of all, bags of bread and chips.

A burly white bulldog sat in the driver's seat of the truck, waiting for his owner to return. When he looked the other way, Myra swooped past him, perching gingerly on the bed rail of the truck bed, her wings flapping to keep her steady. To her immense delight, sitting like a crown jewel on top of the groceries, was a square pink cardboard box with a clear cellophane window on top. Centered neatly inside, was an enormous cake covered with thick white frosting and a generous blend of cranberry and orange candy sprinkles.

Zak watched Myra flutter about from his place on the roof of an empty store. The building had formerly housed a thriving retail outlet for a major appliance chain, but had stood empty for three years. Now it was nothing more than a blemish on the face of the otherwise flourishing shopping center. Sneering at Myra and her obvious delight at finding the cake, he turned away from her so she could not see his face.

"Almost too fat to fly, aren't ya!" he croaked into the wind that dispersed his snickering remark before it could reach its target.

"Say something, old man?" a young raven, flying past, taunted Zak.

Fluttering down to the ground, Zak tucked his beak tightly under his wing and backed tightly into a shadowed corner, ignoring all but his own comfort. He hated the cold, but this place was out of the wind and offered some protection from the fog that blanketed the area. It also kept him away from the other ravens, like the young one that had just heckled him.

It bothered Zak that the younger ravens didn't 'get it'. To him they seemed shallow and devoid of any real integrity or appreciation for the good lives they had. In his mind, they had known none of the strife or sacrifice that marked his own generation. He was glad he had chosen to forego family life, even though he had come close to falling in love once with a beautiful raven he met during the oil spill clean-up. It had been serious for a while, but when things started looking too comfortable, he had driven her off. Even he didn't know why he chased the beautiful bird from his life. Though he knew he had missed his opportunity for happiness with her, he was glad she at least had found it with someone else. As much as the old Zak wanted it to work with her, he knew that the current Zak lacked the capacity to focus on what was needed to nurture the relationship. Hollow since the oil spill, he was consumed with thoughts of what his life could have been had he not been there to experience the devastation that day. Now he saw everyday life as trite. The worries, rituals and joys that marked normal existence, paled in comparison to his own all-consuming thoughts of the tragedy that had overtaken his reality. These intrusive thoughts seeped into his consciousness like the oil spill itself had seeped into the rocky beaches of Prince William Sound. No amount of clean-up, no amount of time was ever going to cleanse his mind and return him to the simpler existence he had known before the spill.

Some of the birds Zak hung out with in the berry trees had mated before. Many had since abandoned their nests, leaving their mates and their hatchlings to fend for themselves. Zak was glad that, as far as he knew, he hadn't been responsible for any of this younger generation of ravens who seemed so lacking in his eyes. Judging by the number of mated ravens who frequented the berry trees in favor of staying in their nests and raising their families, it looked like he wasn't missing too much by not having a family of his own, anyway.

He nestled more tightly into the corner of the building and forced his mind to stop thinking. Later, after a bit, he would fly across town to meet a few of his friends in one of the few trees that had not yet lost its fruit to the cold. Right now, though, he was just killing time.

Pulling the cover of the pink box open with her beak, Myra called in Ravenspeak, inviting the others to join her. Hatchmates Hildie, Lollie, Em-ella, and Zawna flew over. Positioning themselves alongside Myra in a circle around the cake, they gently pecked small pieces out of the tasty dessert, flew off to enjoy each morsel, and then returned for more. How delighted they were to have found such a treat. Happily, they ate away, not noticing the sunlight dimming, filtered by approaching ice fog.

Without warning, Zak darted out of the mist directly to the old Ford, catching Myra off guard and causing her to duck and cower out of fear he would crash into her. Flying straight up, he circled the truck a couple of times. Swooping down, again, he scooped up a beak full of frosting, leaving a deep groove down the center of the cake.

Just as Zak became airborne again, Lloyd, the owner of the pick-up, came walking out carrying his last bag of groceries. Seeing all the ravens gathered around the half-eaten cake, he set his grocery bag on the hood and started waving his arms to shoo the ravens away. Inside the truck, first one dog and then a second jumped up from the seat and started fiercely barking, leaving slobber streaks all over the windows.

"Wishbone! Yty! Sit!" Lloyd barked at his dogs before picking up the mess of cake and tossing it into a nearby dumpster. A flurry of flight sent the ravens airborne in all directions, all except Myra, who was sitting on the edge of the dumpster licking frosting off her wings after climbing out of the cake that Lloyd had just tossed. Obviously, by the surprised look on his face, he had not seen her lying in the middle of it when he picked it up. Myra saw him grab a towel and pour some bottled water on it. Looking concerned, Lloyd took a few steps her way, but he was held back by the dozens of ravens that swooped down around her and began pecking the frosting off her wings to help clean her feathers of the mess.

"Danged birds! How was I supposed to see ya in the middle of that mess?" Lloyd sputtered. Grabbing an ice scraper, he shaved the thick frost off his windows before putting the last bag of groceries inside. Starting up the engine, he drove off, spewing a frozen cloud of exhaust out behind him as he turned out onto the highway to head home.

Zak watched the birds twitter about Myra from his perch on a nearby light pole. Idly, he preened his feathers, chortling mockingly that the frosting-covered Myra was the alleged "white raven." A couple of young ravens were looking his way, laughing. Zak laughed back, wondering why the prank hadn't felt as good as it used to. He looked at the juveniles and cawed another laugh. It sounded hollow to his ears, but he didn't let the younger ravens see his empty expression as he cawed again.

The young ravens cawed back and flapped and fluttered on the ground below, looking up at Zak as their jocularity spread among the others. Soon, a large hoard of birds had gathered at the light pole beneath Zak. With false bravado, he extended one wing and cocked his head; then strutted about on the top of the light box. He was quite unaware that the white frosting mustache on his beak was what had prompted all the laughter.

Chapter Three

Perilous Travel

The holiday shoppers, sensing the upcoming weather change, began to move out of the stores in large numbers. Word had spread quickly that bad weather was rolling in. Burdened with bags and parcels, they glanced anxiously skyward as they scurried to their vehicles. Traffic backed up at the gas pumps as drivers stopped to fill up for the journey home. While they waited for their turn at the pump, some pulled out bottles of glass cleaner and rolls of paper towels from the road kits they carried, using the free moment to clean the headlamps and taillights of their vehicles. By the looks of weather conditions, they were going to need all the help they could get in their travels tonight.

The ravens, sated from their afternoon feast at the dumpsters, began to disappear from the open, seeking protection from both the traffic and the weather. By closing time, the parking lots of the shopping centers in the Valley were a ghost land of empty spaces and the dumpsters held only skeletal remains of the bounty upon which the ravens had feasted.

Lloyd had been one of the first to leave. He sat

waiting at a red light on the outskirts of town with the passenger side window rolled down far enough for both Wishbone and Yty to stick their heads out the window and look around. Exhaust from the tailpipe of the old Ford wound around the rear bumper and alongside the truck, creeping in a heavy, gray mass that left the air smelling of diesel. To Lloyd's left was a jacked-up late model black pick-up with windows tinted so darkly that he could not see how many people were inside. He knew somebody was, by the boom of music that pounded his ears, rocking the truck and everything around it with its vibration. On his right was a small rusty red sedan with one blue fender and a set of nearly bald, mismatched tires. A bumper sticker that read *Peace* covered the upper edge of the driver's side window. Sitting inside was a twenty-something young man who looked, unblinking, straight ahead. Covering his head of unkempt hair was a striped knit cap that had earflaps hanging down like dog ears and ties that dangled their pom pom ends over his collar. Jutting from the back seat were a pair of skis and two poles.

When the light finally changed to green, the vehicles on each side of Lloyd turned onto the crossroad from their respective lanes. With one going right, and the other left, they left Lloyd in the only truck moving away from town. In the rearview mirror, he could see lines of vehicle stacking up behind him as the light turned red again, assuring him he would not be alone on the road for long.

In the rush to get home, no one noticed the ravens huddled in out-of-the-way groups on the ground. Barely visible in the thick mist, they were as efficiently hidden away as they had been conspicuous all afternoon. The air was still except for the noise made by traffic. No sounds came from the birds at all. It was as if they had never been there.

As night descended upon the Valley, the fog continued to thicken, causing slick road conditions, and slowing the bumper-to-bumper holiday traffic to a near crawl. For several hours, vehicles inched one by one out of the parking lots onto the roads for the slow ride back home. Their lights dimmed by the fog, formed a long caravan as they snaked behind Lloyd on the darkened highway.

Lloyd found the narrow, winding Glenn Highway north of Palmer to be particularly harrowing that night, as he made his way to his home near Sheep Mountain. Once he had traveled beyond Sutton, there were no streetlights to help him navigate in the dark. Not even houses or businesses existed to help light up the way, a situation made worse by the lack of moonlight, absence of snow, and by the steep incline of the mountains that rose straight up where the road had been carved through them.

The fog reduced visibility to near zero. As he inched his way along, he muttered under his breath that no holiday was worth this kind of hassle. Shuffling some papers around on the seat and repositioning himself for comfort, he grabbed the steering wheel tightly and barked at his dogs to keep a lookout and help him drive. Wishbone raised one eyebrow and looked blankly at his owner before shifting his position on the seat and falling back asleep beside Yty.

Lloyd never saw the semi-truck go over the guardrail just past Caribou Creek. Landing tipped on its side at the bottom of the canyon, its rear doors had flung open during its tumble down the mountain, spilling most of its contents about. Neither did he see the driver climb up over the guardrail and flag down a truck that had come along behind, or the truck's taillights as it turned back and headed for the city. It had taken him four hours to get home from a trip that usually took only two. When he pulled into his driveway around ten p.m., he quickly unloaded the groceries, plugged in the head bolt heater on his truck and shuttled his dogs into the house, telling them that tonight they could sleep inside.

"Ain't fit for man or beast and surely not for my travelin' partners," he told them, pulling a couple of tin pans he used for dog dishes down off the shelf, and filling them from the crumpled bag of dog food stashed behind a broom in the corner of his kitchen. He filled a third bowl with fresh water and set it down for his pets.

"Don't get too used to it though. Soon as the weather clears, I'm puttin' ya back outdoors in your kennel," he told them.

Tonight, though, the dogs would sleep next to him and he would count himself fortunate that they had all made it back home in one piece.

The newspaper never got there the next morning, but it did the morning after that. It was then that Lloyd read about the accident. According to the story told by the driver who, unhurt, had hitched a ride into Palmer, he had unexpectedly come upon a curve in the fog. This had caused him to skid on a patch of black ice as he tried to navigate it, sending his truck right over the guardrail. The truck cab had come to rest about twenty-five feet down the embankment, held in place by a thick stand of brush alongside a relatively flat outcropping of rock. The trailer, though, had come loose and flipped onto its side, sliding down the bank until coming to rest some four hundred feet down where it wedged itself in a ravine. Crews had gone out the next day and been able to pull out the truck cab and tow it back into Palmer, but any hope of retrieving the trailer and its contents was nil.

The residents of the area, accustomed to such mishaps, had turned out in full force to salvage the goods. It was common knowledge in the area that the trucking companies would not try to retrieve any lost merchandise. These types of accidents were all too common in the harrowing mountain passes in winter, and any attempt to recover the load would be too dangerous and costly to make it worth the effort. The local people knew that the contents of the trailer were free for the taking to anyone who had the inclination to risk their life retrieving them.

Forming a caravan of all-terrain vehicles the

morning after the accident, several locals headed for the trailer. Traveling crosswise across the mountainous terrain and creating a series of switchbacks, they moved along the steep landscape easily. Used to hauling moose, goat, and sheep carcasses from hunting expeditions out of the area, they knew how to navigate the brush-covered rocky slopes and cut a safe trail.

According to one of the men, as quoted in the article in the paper, they had arrived within hours after first light. Except for a few scattered torn bags of dog food and a smattering of plastic pet toys, the trailer was empty. They had passed a wolf pack on the way and fired off several shots to chase them away. Even though there was a bounty on the animals right now, they didn't want to have to bother with tracking and skinning at the expense of their real mission of reaching the overturned trailer. Fresh paw prints were evident all around the open bags of dog food, but there was no other sign that anyone or anything but the wolves had been near the trailer. Never in all the years of scavenging these accidents had any of them ever known a semi to travel with a half-empty trailer like this, especially in the bad weather that had prevailed. The strangeness of this discovery would be the talk of the area for some time to come, especially since the truck driver had stated to officials that he had been traveling with a full load; a fact verified by weigh station records on file.

Big Jim Kaye, a loner of a man and a competent dog-musher, was more surprised than even the rest. The last year had been rough on both him and his dog team, leaving him with bouts of both exhaustion and despair. Injuries during last year's sled dog race had kept him from earning enough money for adequate feed for his dogs and he had taken to rationing what little food he had left. Many days, the pain from his injuries was so bad that he could barely get out of bed, but each day he made himself get up and try to have a normal life. In a moment of good fortune, he had managed to shoot a moose that wandered nearby and had spent the better part of two weeks harvesting the meat from the carcass he had dragged with his ATV to a shed on his property. Once the job was done, he used the ATV to drag the remnants of the carcass well away from his homestead to keep away the bears and other scavengers that would finish it off. He had even been able to store the meat in a food cache he maintained on the property, and had since used most of the meat to feed both himself and his dogs.

He had found suitable homes for over half his dogs, but struggled to maintain the rest until he could either heal or find someone to care for them. No one in the area needed more dogs and Jim was not one to stoop to shooting those he couldn't care for, as was the unspoken rule for many who found themselves in a position of having too many canine mouths to feed. Exhausted from doing more work than he was physically able to tolerate, he had been holed up recovering for the last month. Now he was running out of firewood and still lacked the endurance to go out and chop down a couple of trees and haul them home to cut and split. A proud man, just yesterday he had done the unthinkable and asked for help from some of the guys that hung out at the only restaurant in the area. It had taken him two weeks of hard thinking to talk himself into using what little gas he had left to ride his ATV up to the restaurant and reveal his plight. Assuring the locals that this was just a temporary setback and promising to return the favor as soon as he was on his feet again, he had convinced himself to let them come to his homestead later this week and cut the wood he needed to get by.

Back home by nightfall, he had gone to bed feeling defeated. He had always been a man of re-sourcefulness. Bearing an independent nature and a disciplined work ethic, he had easily been able to live a subsistence lifestyle. Worried, now, about how he would feed his dogs, and embarrassed at having to beg for help with his firewood, he slept fitfully before falling into a deep sleep in the wee hours of the morning. When he awoke hours after the sun had come up, he wandered out to the dog lot surprised to find all of his animals asleep inside their barrels. The absence of the dog's usual frenzied howl for breakfast had failed to wake him up at daybreak. With paws over noses, the dogs were the picture of contentment. Food dishes sat empty in front of each barrel, some with a few nuggets of dry food remaining uneaten. Strange, since Big Jim Kaye always fed his dogs a concoction of moose meat stew that he cooked up in huge batches every few days. Yesterday he had served his team the last of the stew and left their cleaned-out bowls empty when he went to bed, hoping to make it into town in the morning and barter some silver he had stashed away for some kibble.

Something in the corner of the dog lot caught his attention. Walking closer, he saw bag after bag of empty dog food sacks stacked neatly in one corner of the yard. There were stacks of still unopened bags in another. Wondering how they could possibly have gotten there, he searched for tire tracks or footprints or any sign that someone had come by to deliver them, and found none. What he did find, though, was one blue-black feather with white tipped edges lying on the ground amidst the footprints of scores of birds. Speechless, he made his way back to his cabin, trying to come up with a rational explanation for the bounty left for his dogs. Later, when his neighbors came to cut his wood, he asked them about the strange occurrence. They told him they were as mystified as he was and related the story of the accident and the near-empty trailer that had left all of them scratching their heads in wonder. He thought he saw a couple of them squinting at him when they thought he wasn't looking. Suspicious by nature, some of them habitually seemed to look for the worst. Anyone looking at him, though, could easily see that Big Jim Kaye had neither the energy nor the means to have moved that many bags of dog food from such a remote location in the dead of one of the coldest, foggiest nights on record. Being unable to give reason to the strange occurrence, and too tired to think anymore, he thanked them for the four cords of wood they left stacked near the front of his cabin, went back inside near nightfall and wept with relief.

The story of the mishap at Caribou Creek and the unexplained good fortune of the musher and his dogs became the main topic of discussion at the round table in the local coffee shop. For the next few weeks, several of the local residents tried putting their individual spin on the two biggest events to have occurred in the area in months.

One middle-aged mechanic thought it was rather suspicious that a truck filled with dog food just happened to go off the cliff at the very same time that the musher's dogs were going hungry. Another local felt that it was all just coincidental. One old sourdough miner swore that he had seen several eagles hanging around the dog lot quite regularly as of late. His mining partner, a lean and toothless scruff of a man, just nodded his head and said nothing. Most everyone agreed that, no matter how things had come down, or what questionable force was behind it, Big Jim Kaye was as deserving as anyone else of the free goods. After all, they established, hadn't each and every one of them made out well from these winter truck spills at some time or another?

Wils Kelderman, sitting alone at a nearby table,

listened and quietly took notes, taking particular care to describe the blue-black feather with white edges that had been found near the sacks of dog food.

Meanwhile, as the last leaves fell from the trees and winter days became mostly winter nights, life quietly returned to normal. The locals continued to wake up to the howls of Big Jim Kaye's dogs and they continued to gather at the round table for coffee each morning. There they would sit and stare out over miles of peaks and valleys, discussing the day's events, while the comforting aroma of wood smoke wafted through the air from Big Jim Kaye's cabin down below.

———

Zak heard chatter about the musher, the dog food, and the strange bird prints during several of his flights around the Valley. Even the old regulars at the berry trees were talking about what had happened, prompting Zak to dismiss them with a sneer and start hanging around alone. He was already restless, bored with the darkness and lack of snow. All the hoopla about good deeds and white raven just aggravated his already antisocial mood. Usually he would stop in to grab a few berries and then fly off to a secret place to eat them at his leisure. He liked them because they made him feel good and made everything that usually annoyed him seem funny, funny enough for him to eventually start hanging around his friends again. Sometimes they even made him fly upside down; at least he thought they did. One afternoon, he almost snapped his beak off when he fell on his face trying to pick up a bag of dog food from the back porch of a nearby house, while joking about the incident at Caribou Creek. Another day, he did a back flip off one of the branches, landing with a splat on the ground below.

"Better lay off them berries, old man," one of the younger ravens told him.

"The day I can't have any danged blastin' fun around here is the last day you'll see me in this tree," Zak spat back, retreating to one of the branches and chomping down a couple of more berries.

The truth was that the berries really weren't working that well for him anymore. Hanging out in the berry trees had become more of a chore than a pleasure. He could hardly generate any enthusiasm at all for his traditional noontime raid at the hamburger stand, which made his lunchtime exploits with Ed much less fun. The first major snowfall of the year was later than usual, too, which meant that one of his favorite pastimes of hopping around on snow berms was going to have to wait. Then again, snow berms didn't interest him that much anymore either. They made his feet cold and pulling them up one at a time into his feathers for warmth felt like too much work. Besides, sliding down the icy snow piles hadn't been as much fun lately as it used to be.

Nothing about this winter felt right. He hadn't seen a moose since the end of last April and wondered if the lack of snowfall was keeping them in the high country. He found it bothersome that there seemed to be more fog than usual this year, making visibility poor during the already shortened days, and keeping himself and the other ravens close to the ground. The crowded conditions of the grouped-up ravens were getting on his nerves. He liked the wide-open spaces where he didn't have to listen to their chatter or, worse yet, pretend like he cared about what they were doing. With little else to do, he spent most of his time in the city, drifting from one berry tree to another or, more often than not, tucking himself into some out-of-the-way spot and sleeping.

Zak was tailing an eagle over Cottonwood Lake one day when he saw the white raven for the first time. It was only a glimpse, but it was enough for him to see that it was a raven and it was white. So the others had been right. He was going to need to check this out and find out what the deal was with this great wonder everyone couldn't stop talking about. Breaking free from the thermal he was riding with the eagle, he took off in the direction of the white raven that was now flying just beyond Palmer toward Pioneer Peak. He had it clearly in his sight, and was gaining ground when the gray-ish-white bird turned suddenly, disappearing in the direction of the Knik Glacier.

"There's somethin' fishy about the whole thing," he croaked to his friends back at the berry tree, using a false bravado to conceal his frustration at not having been able to confront the elusive bird.

"More 'n likely some kind of mutant," one of his buddies theorized, "but, if ya got nothin' else to do, might as well check 'er out."

"Might," Zak answered, "and might not."

Over the next few weeks, Zak stopped talking to his buddies about the bird. Every day, he flew over the area along the Knik River Road that led up to the glacier trying to spot a glimpse of it. Each day he saw nothing of the white bird that he was determined to investigate. A couple of times he thought he caught sight of it again, but couldn't be sure. He was getting frustrated by the search and by how easily the bird had evaded someone that was as savvy as he was. He needed to let it go and move on, but thoughts of finding the mysterious bird persisted. Beginning to question why he was searching so hard, he felt annoyed that he even cared.

He did finally see his first moose of the winter. It was an old bull, with a huge rack of antlers that two juvenile ravens seemed determined to use as a resting place. Almost every day, Zak would see the moose with the two ravens sitting on its antlers as it walked about. He envied them, wishing he could quell his mind and live a life of such simple pleasure. Carefree, the two birds slid down the antlers each time the moose lowered its head to feed. Flapping their wings, they always managed to get airborne just before hitting the ground. The moose, unbothered by their antics, remained an unmindful accessory to their silliness.

Zak wondered how they were able to stay so joyful and live so easily when each one of his own days felt like no more than an unending, tedious existence. He tried to remember a time when he hadn't felt this way. He knew there had been such a time, but it had been so long ago, he couldn't remember when it was, much less what it felt like.

He thought the change in him started right after the oil spill. He remembered wondering then if he had been exposed to some toxic fumes that had affected his mind. Coming back from the beaches, he noticed unpredictable impatience and hostility surfacing in his otherwise playful personality, especially toward humans. He started doing risky things. His old friends called him crazy and some stopped hanging out with him. One of his favorite pastimes became dodging bullets at the big city dump. He had stumbled on the sport unintentionally one day on discovering some of the best food picking in the state right there in the heart of the city. Thinking it great that he no longer had to fly from dumpster to dumpster, he began to indulge in the equivalent of a raven buffet, the city dump.

Sometimes while he was pecking around deep in the trash, his beak would get stuck in the thick plastic that lined the bottom of the dump. The liner had been put there to provide a barrier that prevented seepage of the contents of the dump into the ground. It was during one of those times that the first bullets started zinging just past him. He could see a man in a pick-up truck shooting in his direction from across the dump. At first, Zak thought it was a mistake, but it soon became evident that the man was shooting around him as if he was trying to scare him off. One day he heard the man holler about how the birds were ruining the liner of the dump with all their pecking. In Zak's mind, it was just another example of a human trying to wreak havoc on the lives of birds, just as the one who had caused the oil spill had done.

Zak felt no need to back down from the man with the gun, choosing instead to hassle him right back. He began taunting the hired sniper by flying around right in front of him and then dive-bombing deep into the garbage pile. Sometimes he pretended that his beak was stuck just to get the man's attention. When the warning shots fired, Zak would deliberately make a point of pecking harder and harder at the contents. Ultimately, his defiance would lead to the man shooting with more accuracy, prompting Zak to dive and swoop to avoid the bullets. He became skillful at evasive tactics and more emboldened each day, much to the consternation of the dump officials.

"Mess with me and I'll mess back," he cawed as he flew.

Before long, Zak had become so skilled at dodging bullets that he found the game unchallenging. That was when he invited several of his friends to join him. A lot of them did, but found the game too harrowing and went on to other things. One good friend named Mackie stuck around. He looked up to Zak and wanted to learn everything Zak knew about taunting humans and dodging bullets. Zak was more than happy to serve as Mackie's mentor, and teach him all he knew about messing with the humans who took themselves so seriously; they made messing with them easy.

For weeks on end, the two ravens ramped up their activities at the dump, even coming at night, which was not their usual feeding pattern. They were getting by on less and less sleep in order to pursue their little game. Sometimes Zak felt as though his reflexes were slowing a bit, but after a couple of swoops, he was usually right up to speed.

On the last day that he visited the dump, Zak was having an especially frenzied interaction with the man in the pick-up truck. Another man was there this time, helping the regular bird-sniper. As usual, Zak taunted the men for a couple of hours before instigating a serious outburst of gunfire. This day, he felt especially proud of himself for having mastered a figure eight flight pattern that allowed him to dodge bullets from both guns at once. Giddy with bravado, he flew faster and swooped deeper, not realizing that Mackie was tailing him tightly behind. Suddenly, after a rapid burst of gunfire, the shooting stopped. When Zak turned his head to see what was up, he saw Mackie fall, motionless, to the ground. Darting downward to check on his friend, he was driven off by a barrage of gunfire. From a place on the edge of the tall fence that surrounded the dump, he saw the man pick Mackie up by the tail and throw his limp form into the rubbish.

Sickened beyond anything he had ever felt before, Zak flew in, trying to retrieve Mackie, but the gunfire resumed, forcing him to fly off again. Later, he flew back over and saw Mackie still laying the way he had fallen when thrown, his neck cocked unnaturally out of alignment, and one wing flung out beside him. He knew then, that it had all been his fault. If not for his irresponsible thrill-seeking, Mackie would still be alive. Wracked with guilt for bringing his friend to harm's way, he told himself he was a loser. He couldn't imagine he was ever going to be able to forgive himself or love himself again. Then, without warning, he felt the anger and frustration that had surfaced after the oil spill return.

"It's your own fault, Mackie. You should have never listened to me," Zak screeched across the dump, unable to deal with the enormity of what had just happened. Turning and flying away, he pushed all thoughts of Mackie and any further interest in the dump out of his head.

A few days later, certain that he had spotted the white raven, Zak took off in the direction of the glacier, turning back halfway up the Knik Valley after losing sight of the bird again. On his way back, he noticed a larger than usual number of ravens gathered on the gravel bar in the middle of the river, just south of the old bridge. Low-lying fog blanketed most of the river, but he was able to count at least thirty raven silhouettes on the sandbar. It was so unusual, that he even commented about it later to one of his pals in the berry tree, where he had resumed spending most of his free time.

The people of the region were as impatient as Zak and the ravens were with the delayed onset of winter. Although the snow-free roads seemed preferable to the slushy alternative, frequent incoming fog banks made the highways icy and driving precarious. With only a few hours of daylight and no real sun to warm the pavement, driving conditions remained tricky a good part of the time.

The lack of snowfall also made the area along Knik River Road and other side roads close to the mountains, darker than usual. This area, where the sun did little more than crest the mountaintops for the entire winter, was more affected than most by the darkness. The bare frozen ground reflected so little light that it made it hard to see the shadowy silhouette of dangers, such as moose, along the highways. This year the darkness was worse than ever, prompting people to stay inside and the ravens flock to places on the ground.

These prevailing weather conditions also made the winter seem longer. Hunkered down inside their homes, immersed in hobbies and pastimes, people felt more than the usual jolt to their senses when *the snow finally did arrive and they had to face the elements outside.*

———

The snow began falling in earnest the fourth morning of December. Inside the Pioneer Home for long-time Alaska residents and veterans, William D was dozing in a rocking chair alongside the only window in his room. Having reached the grand age of one hundred, he tired easily and napped often. When he was awake, though, he talked often of a long life; a life that by most standards could be judged well lived.

William D loved his room. It faced east and had a clear view of the Knik Glacier and the surrounding mountains. Failing eyesight prevented him from seeing much more than shapes and shadows, but he was still able to enjoy the brightness of the sunrise and the silhouette of the mountains each morning. Each day he walked with the help of his cane down the long hallway to the dining room. There he joined the other residents at eight for breakfast and again at noon and six for lunch and dinner respectively. During breakfast each day, he usually managed to tuck a little bit of his meal into the pocket of his sweater, pretending to save it for a morning snack.

Right on schedule, William D would excuse himself from the others in the dining hall, go to his room, crank open his window, and feed the ravens bits of toast and jam that he saved from his breakfast. William D would bring enough food for all the birds, enough to last until Zak finally arrived. The fact that Zak made it there at all was nothing short of a testament to his love for William D and the kindness he had always bestowed on the errant raven. Everyone knew that Zak was William D's favorite by the way William D always saved him the last bite of food.

Zak liked that William D looked after him and fed him. He knew he could always count on the old man. It made him feel safe, like there was something good in the world he could depend on. William D would always chuckle at the way Zak took the last morsel from his hand.

"There you go, hungry fella," he would say. "That'll tide you over for another day."

The nurses and care attendants all knew what was going on and made sure to keep William D's window open just a tad so he wouldn't have to work too hard to open it up. They also made sure to cover his shoulders with his old brown wool army blanket to keep him from getting a chill. Although the blanket was thin and worn, William D felt comforted by the way it wrapped around him. Just as it had for the last seventy-five or so years of his life, it had a familiar smell and imparted a familiar comfort that made him feel good. Almost every Christmas he would open another gift package from one of his children or grandchildren. Almost every Christmas he would give the new comforter that was inside to one of the other residents in the home, telling his family that the other person needed it more than he did.

After eating, Zak and several other ravens would sit on the windowsill with feathers fluffed for warmth to keep a draft from the window until William D fell asleep in his chair. Those that couldn't fit on the sill gathered on the ground below, making it easy for passersby to spot William D's room among the row of others in the building. His family, among those going about their daily errands in this small town, always knew that if the ravens were there, that William D was safely asleep in his chair for his morning nap. Later in the day, the ravens would fly off only to return again the next morning.

On this particular fourth morning of December, none of the nurses saw the white raven sitting on the windowsill in the newly falling snow as William D slept in his room and Zak slept on the windowsill outside. Neither did the cleaning lady who straightened his room or the dietician who stopped by to see if William D was getting enough to eat. Once Zak thought he heard something stir nearby, but when he lazily opened one eye and looked around, he saw nothing but some leaves blowing around in the wind.

Lately, William D had been thinking a lot about his granddaughter, Sophie, who was soon to give birth to her first child and William D's first great-grandchild. While he slept, he dreamed of her and the little baby he would soon hold in his arms.

This day, while her grandfather slept in his

rocking chair as usual, the snow began falling. At the same time, in a cabin near the top of Lazy Mountain just north of Palmer, Sophie felt her labor begin in earnest. She placed a phone call to her husband, Donald, around ten a.m., leaving a message for him at work that she was on her way down the mountain to the hospital. It was eleven a.m. before Donald finished teaching his history class at the high school and got the message. He immediately tried to call her, but there was no answer on her cell phone. This was not unusual, since the mountain road sometimes blocked the transmission signal needed for the message to go through. Concerned about the heavy snow that was now coming down, he called the hospital only to learn that Sophie had not yet arrived. Canceling his classes for the day before jumping into his pick-up, he headed straight for the only road up Lazy Mountain. William D, asleep in his chair, and Zak, asleep outside on the windowsill, knew nothing of Sophie's plight, nor did they notice the other ravens fly off in the direction of Lazy Mountain.

It was snowing heavily and there were already six inches of fresh snow on the dark, winding mountain road. Donald made it halfway up to the ninety-degree curve before a roadblock stopped him. Three cars were piled in the gulley-like ditch to the right and four others were jackknifed across both lanes of the road. One by one, troopers directed drivers to back around and head back down the mountain. Unlike the others, who were backing around in a

U-shaped turn and going back down the mountain, Donald sat there waiting to reach the head of the line. When the trooper approached his vehicle and tried to get him to turn around, he rolled down his window and explained that his wife was coming down the mountain with a baby on the way.

Directing him to a safe place to wait, the trooper checked all seven vehicles, returning to tell him that his wife was not among the injured. Relieved that Sophie was not involved in the accident, Donald prayed as he struggled to come up with a plan that would help him reach his wife and get her down the mountain and safely to the hospital. Driving up to the first house he saw that had a snowmobile outside, he frantically asked the owner for help. Within minutes, he and a sixty-something guy named Rich were speeding on the snow machine up a back way.

Rich told Donald that he had lived on the mountain for close to thirty years. Although he said he knew it like he knew the back of his hand, the snow was coming down so hard that they soon lost track of the road they had been running alongside of while they searched for Sophie. On top of the blinding snow, nightfall was coming on, making their own safety as urgent as was their search for Sophie. Just as they were about to turn and follow their trail back down to Rich's home, the ravens began to appear. One by one, they fluttered past the two men before landing in the snow ahead, hopping one over the other to form markers in the snow. Instinctively, the men followed them. For the better part of an hour, the ravens formed a black-feathered trail that stopped when they reached Sophie's car. They found Sophie huddled inside, wrapped in one of the blankets Donald had long insisted she carry. In her arms, all pink and soft and warm was their new baby.

Zak, who had heard about the raven trail and had flown up Lazy Mountain in spite of the storm to see for himself, watched from high in a tree. He saw six ravens sitting on top of Sophie's car with their wings spread out as if in a protective umbrella of feathers to keep the snow from piling on top. For a moment he started to join them, turning away at the last minute and flying back to a place where he liked to hide on the riverbank. He told himself that Sophie and the baby were all right. He let himself imagine how happy William D would be. He tried to convince himself not to feel guilty for turning away when he had been close enough to lend the other ravens a wing to help Donald and Sophie. He gave himself mental points for at least having the conscience to feel bad about it. Then he went to sleep so he wouldn't have to think anymore.

"She's here," William D told the nurse who nudged him awake for his pills.

"Why, who do you mean?" the nurse replied, tucking William D's blanket down around his knees.

"Baby girl Louisa Anne," William D answered.

Closing his eyes, he went back to finish his nap. It was no surprise when the phone rang at five p.m., and the nurse walked down the hall and woke him to tell him that Sophie and baby girl Louisa Anne were safe at the hospital.

"I know," he said with a smile.

As word of the birth of William D's great-grand-daughter spread throughout the Pioneer Home, residents gathered in his room to congratulate him. Later, a nurse brought the baby and Sophie in a wheelchair to his room. Some of the ladies counted her fingers and toes, assuring William D that every-thing was all right once they had accomplished this age-old motherly tradition. Bundling the baby back up in her blanket, a couple of them noticed a white-edged black feather lying inside and mentioned it to Sophie and the nurse. No one could explain how it got there. No one, that is, except for William D, who just nodded with a knowing smile.

The next morning, Zak showed up later than usual at William D's window. As usual, William D had saved the last bite for him.

"I knew you'd come," he said, reaching his fingers under a crack in the window to feed a piece of toast to his favorite raven. Zak hesitated before taking the morsel and swallowing it down. He had never known a man as kind and loving as William D and this feeling touched him in a way that he hadn't felt in a very long time.

William D reached under the window to hand Zak another piece of toast, but this time Zak hopped backwards and lowered his head, not taking the bite he told himself he didn't deserve.

"Come on, now, little guy," William D said, coaxing Zak back to his fingers.

"You go ahead and eat that, now," William D said.

Zak fluttered his wings in preparation for flight and started to lift himself off the windowsill. Lowering himself back down, he looked at William D who, despite the freezing temperatures, still held his fingers out with the piece of toast for the bird.

"Come on, now," William D said. "Come get this so you don't go hungry."

Still Zak hesitated, prompting William D to shake his head mumbling, "Tsk tsk tsk, do you think I don't know how you feel?"

Zak took the piece of toast from William D's trembling fingers and began pecking at it with his beak. It tasted good and he savored it.

"There you go, now. It's all right. You just enjoy that, my friend. One thing I learned long ago –and you'll learn it, too –is that sometimes the giving is in the taking," William D told Zak, before pulling his brown blanket up close to his shoulders and nodding off to sleep.

As the long nights slid into lengthening days, many people of the Mat-Su Valley began venturing outdoors more often than they had during the preceding two darkest months of the year. The weather was colder now, remaining consistently well below freezing. Aside from the dirt used to sand the roads for better traction, Alaska was a wonderland of icy white wonder. With the holidays behind them and no end to winter near, residents began to look for the beauty unveiled by the emerging sun.

Couples, mostly, could be seen driving up the long winding road toward Knik Glacier. There was something about this road that attracted them. Perhaps it had something to do with the fact that it led nowhere, except to the top of a gently ascending slope where it ended at a school bus turnaround. Perhaps it was the area's reputation for being both a wildlife corridor and a place populated with those who led a mostly subsistence lifestyle. Whatever the reason, during the winter when the tourists were gone, the local people came.

Here, there was a quietness not found in the city. A pristine solitude that made one feel melded with nature. It was a place where drivers slowed to crane their necks at every For Sale *sign and jumped out to retrieve real estate flyers in hopes that they were one of the few able to find an affordable piece of land so close to the real Alaska. Here, within driving distance of civilization, could be found a replenishing respite from city noises. Whatever its appeal, people drove lazily on this road, often stopping right in the center of it to take a picture if they saw something that moved them. It was a peaceful spot where people turned up their car heaters and opened their sunroofs in the sub-zero weather to watch the northern lights dance when darkness came.*

Early one January morning, Zak perched alone on top of the old trestle bridge that led over the wide silty glacier-fed Knik River. He liked this place and lately had been coming here often. Something about being in this area gave him peace, at least as much peace as he had been able to find. He found that gazing at the lush valley displaced the thoughts of the oil spill and Mackie's death that kept creeping into his consciousness. The deep turquoise of the Knik Glacier stood against the landscape as though a jewel on the horizon. It mesmerized him and took some of the pain away.

He watched the silhouette of one lone raven fly east toward the glacier. A couple of ravens who landed on the bridge watched with him.

"There goes Maya off to seek her future," one said to the other as the two birds took flight.

"I heard she is joining the young raven named True," the other responded.

"How do you think you know these things?" Zak squawked in the direction of their receding tail feathers.

He strutted back and forth along the top rail of the bridge trying to regain the sense of solitude that the two ravens had disturbed. Facing the glacier again, he watched the young raven the others had called Maya. Flying above the ice fog that had settled over the valley, she followed the path of the river led by a streak of sparkling white. With each flap of her wings, the fog lifted, revealing the valley below. Now covered in shimmering frost, it glimmered like billions of diamonds in the sun. Swooping low, nearly to the valley floor, Maya touched wings with the raven called True who had lifted in flight from a rock in the river. Together, wing tips almost touching, the two ravens rose from the heart of the valley.

Zak was unable to take his eyes off the two young ravens in flight. How beautiful they were. How pure the love that guided them to their destiny. Zak took flight and followed, staying back so he wouldn't disturb them. Awed, he flew behind, following them to see where they were going. Only the soft wingstrokes of their flight broke the silence as they journeyed into the night. Too entranced by the scene before him to look away, he lost track of time.

Then he saw it appear. Spellbound, he watched the scene unfolding before him. Nothing had prepared him for this moment at this time as he watched the white raven lead Maya and True through the crystal night. He felt his heart, separated for so long from his soul, beat as if it would fly from his chest. The feeling caught him off guard, almost causing him to forget to fly. For a moment, he thought he might fall from the sky, but he remembered to beat his wings before he did. Immense joy overwhelmed his senses, making him wonder if it were all a dream. For a moment, he wanted to flee, to find a berry tree, and wake up from this fantasy; but there were no such trees near the glacier, and the thought vanished. He started to fly downward to a rock in the river, but the sight of the young Maya and True led by the white raven, the parting of the fog and the revelation of the sparkling valley below, lifted him up. Wrapped in the warmth of awareness, everything suddenly made sense. The overturned truck, the dog food, Sophie's birth, William D's kind understanding, the ravens gathering on the gravel bar and the fog had all been the white raven trying to reunite Zak's own suffering soul with the love buried deep in his heart.

Zak saw his reflection in an icy, moonlit pond below and saw the miracle unfold. First, the tips of his wings, then his tail, his head and all of his body turned a glimmering white. Covered as though with frost, he was dazzling. In spite of his icy appearance, he radiated a warm inner glow that made his feathers shimmer as though covered in crushed diamonds. Soaring over the pond, he watched his reflection, astounded. Almost as quickly as they had turned white, his feathers returned to their natural black color. He cocked his head to look at himself. His feathers were definitely black. When he looked down in the ice of the pond, the reflection there was black now, too, but Zak was not the same. He felt lighter now, more free. The sense of peace and warmth had unburdened his soul. He looked ahead at the white raven leading Maya and True to their destiny and he began to understand. The white raven lived within all ravens, and it lived within him.

In revealing the purity of her love for True, Maya had awakened the inner light that shined deep in Zak's heart. It had touched him and opened his heart in a way he had not known for some time. He felt strengthened by the goodness before him as his fears and struggles faded in the light of his newfound awareness. At that moment, Zak forgave himself, not for anything he had done, but for allowing his troubles to nearly suffocate his inner light.

"You nearly threw your life away on berry trees and anger," he admonished himself.

"You only felt the pain so deeply because you cared so deeply," he heard a voice say.

It was the white raven!

He caught another glimpse of the white raven that had spoken, and flew in a circle trying to catch up with it. Was it around him? Behind him? Under him? He darted about trying to catch it before he remembered that the white raven was inside him, just as it was inside all ravens. The voice he had heard, the voice of the white raven, was his own. Nothing would ever take away the memories of the events that had troubled Zak for so long, but he knew now that he had to love himself and forgive himself before he could begin to relieve the pain. He felt the veil lift from his troubled heart and he felt the flame of hope flicker to life once again. He realized that his inner light was one that needed to be nourished and protected in order to give him the strength he needed to survive what he had been through. So long consumed by the tragedies he had faced, he had forgotten to give breath to the very essence of his soul. Immersed in the tragedies that had befallen him, he had forgotten how to love himself. Amazed that the light in his heart still flickered underneath the pain and hurt heaped upon it, he vowed never to let it fade again.

Zak watched as Maya and True flew over the glacier. He watched their wings dusting the translucent blue ice with snow sparkles as they followed a moonbeam into the night. In the stillness around him, Zak glided over the valley transformed. Alone now, he hovered in the quiet valley while tiny ice crystals fell from the air. He tasted the crystal's refreshing coolness on his tongue and felt it fall gently on his wings. Watching as it rolled back in to fill the wake created by Maya and True, he felt the ice fog wrap him in its peaceful embrace.

As January moved into February, locals continued to journey up the frozen road that ran alongside the river to Knik Glacier. This year, ravens seemed to be everywhere along the icy river valley. A white coating of frost tinged the feathers of many of them, making them look as though one with the landscape. Many Valley residents could think of no more beautiful a place than this as they enjoyed the unspoiled vistas. Each day grew longer as the sun began to move higher on the horizon, bringing with it the promise of spring. In the brightening light of the shortest month of the year, February drew to a close.

When March arrived, it brought with it a southerly wind and unusually balmy weather. Enticed by the promise of spring, people began to find reasons to spend more time outdoors. Some, in the folly of rash preparedness, even brought out garden hoses and rakes to begin readying themselves for summer. The rapidly melting frost and ice made this period, known as 'breakup' in Alaska, arrive earlier than usual. The effects of the early warming were also more intense than usual this year. Slushy potholes in the road's winter icepack rattled both vehicles and *their occupants as people spent more and more time driving about. Puddled in pond-sized proportions on still frozen ground, rapidly melting snow exposed the dreary brown mess of the dormant earth. The warm promise of spring was beginning to feel like a cruel taunt after the long winter. Everyone knew that in spite of what the thermometer said, winter was far from over.*

The wind began midday on a March Sunday, blew without respite into the next Sunday and halfway into the week beyond. As the roaring engine of the storm rumbled toward the Valley, the tree's tiniest branches began to quiver in advance of the dust cloud sweeping down the two large glaciers to the east. Within minutes after the first twig trembled in advance of the approaching storm, the tree's trunks strained to remain upright against the onslaught of frigid hurricane force wind; their branches lashing wildly in the vortex around them.

The balmy, spring-like temperatures that had prevailed for the past two weeks plunged to zero and below when the wind shifted and spiraled down the glaciers catching everyone in the Valley off guard. Its deafening roar sent both people and animals scurrying for shelter.

Although strong winds were a frequent occurrence in the area, nothing like this had happened in anyone's memory. Gusts, with a sustained force exceeding one hundred miles per hour, blasted everything in their path with sand, old volcanic ash and silt from the beds of nearby glacier-fed rivers. The raging wind ripped holes in roofs, broke out windows, and sent sheets of metal roofing flying through the air. The few people who dared to brave the elements found themselves forced to drive erratically to dodge the flying debris. Once at their destinations, they found it impossible to move about outdoors without anchoring themselves to objects like steel railings and cement walls that were grounded solidly to the earth. Even as they reached the safety of buildings, many found heavy exterior doors ripped from their hands as they tried to enter, leaving hinges sprung and glass shattered in the wake of the winds fury.

Zak, sitting quietly in a place of peace he had found near the Knik Glacier was jolted from his notch in a hollow beneath a stand of spruce trees. Since February, he had been spending most of his time here. In this place where his heart had been re-awakened and his inner light re-kindled, he found comfort.

Something about the wind on this particular day alarmed him. Inexplicably restless now, his mind flooded with the same sensations of doom he had experienced after the oil spill. Nervously, he flew out from under the trees. The wind in its fury jettisoned him backwards against them. Somehow, he managed to get back under the safety of the branches. Trembling, he froze in a state between the need to flee and the fear of moving. Trees bent to the ground as he watched. Branches, torn loose by the wind, flew by all around him. Some of them pinned ravens and other birds to the ground underneath them as they fell.

Wils Kelderman saw the first twitches of the branches from his hiding place behind some bushes across the road from the old trestle bridge. Positioned in the perfect vantage point from which to watch ravens, he tensed at the sound of the roar he recognized as the oncoming wind. He had been through these gusts so common to the Valley before, and had decided that the raven viewing today was too good to abandon just because of a little increase in the air current. Rising from his crouched position, he felt a sharp pain in his left leg. An injury years ago had made his knee lock up when he bent down this way, and resulting arthritis had left him with a noticeable limp. Grabbing for a branch to keep himself from falling, he clumsily knocked his round-rimmed glasses askew. Letting go of the branch to catch them before they could fall to the ground, he stumbled backwards, landing on his hands in the sandy soil. He felt the old bitterness at losing his health insurance to rising costs return, and he cursed into the blast of air that was streaming in his direction. Hadn't it been hard enough to survive on a retiree's meager ration and still pay for his education? He wondered if life would ever become easy for someone as obviously cursed as he. Next year he would be eligible for Medicare, but for now, his debt was overwhelming. Besides, he already knew that the cost for the total knee replacement and ongoing physical therapy that he would need, as well as costs for treatment for his heart condition were well above what Medicare would pay. Reaching back behind his neck with both hands, he tightened the elastic band on the long gray, ponytail that was the only remnant of youth he still enjoyed. He went back to watching the ravens, wondering why he was even there. Who, he told himself, was going to hire a sixty-four year old ornithologist with major health issues, anyway?

***

Backing more tightly against the notch under his favorite tree, Zak sat in his place safe from the wind. In front of him, he saw the devastation unfold. Unable to find shelter as he had, or to control their flight in the blasting force of the wind, the lifeless bodies of ravens, eagles, magpies, and jays lay in every direction, pinned to their deaths by the flying debris. Desperately, he wanted to help those he saw still struggling to fly, but much like the massive oil spill of years ago, he knew he was no match for the force of destruction unwrapping itself before him.

Aware that scores of his raven friends were in an open area of the riverbed below, and knowing that the wind was careening down the glacier directly toward them, Zak struggled to find a way to warn his friends. With no way to reach them in the treacherous winds, he did the only thing he could think of to warn them. Opening his beak, he screamed and then he screamed again. Like a shrill undulating siren of sound, his anguished call joined the wind and reverberated along the canyon walls. Over and over, he screamed, summoning every ounce of strength in his body and every molecule of air in his lungs to blast an alarm to the unsuspecting ravens on the riverbed below. Spent by the effort, he collapsed on the ground and heaved his chest violently in an effort to replenish the air he had forced from his lungs. Pulling himself upright again, he screamed some more, until finally no more sounds came from his throat.

Near the old trestle bridge that spanned the Knik River, waves of ravens driven by the eerie sound, lifted in flight from the riverbank. Flying away from the storm and into the heart of the Valley, they sought protection in the nooks and crannies of the city. There, safely, they rode out the storm.

———·———

Wils Kelderman, too, heard the wail of Zak's screams, and watched as the birds fled, driven by the sound. He barely had time to get inside the safety of his station wagon before the wind bore down, creating a wall of sand that blasted everything in its path, and made it hard to breathe. Leaning back against his car seat safely inside, he heaved a sigh of relief and silently thanked whatever force had created the alarm that saved him from being caught in the storms fury.

Suddenly, Wils no longer felt sorry for himself. Shaking away the despair he had allowed to steal his passion for the study of birds, he fumbled for his voice recorder. Shouting his thoughts above the raging roar of the storm into the handheld device, he described with painstaking accuracy, every intricate behavior he had seen in the ravens before and during their panicked flight. Later he would learn that few others had been fortunate enough to witness ravens fleeing such an event, and fewer still had taken the time to document every detail as he had. The detail in which he described the screaming alarm, and his estimation that it had come from a raven, lent particular significance to his report. Never before had anyone documented such a sound. Then later, as the scope of his work was realized, would he bow his head in humility when they presented him with the highest award granted for this unparalleled achievement. For now, though, he would wait out the storm and then go home.

Zak collapsed and lay almost lifeless under his tree as the storm spewed its force over the Valley for the next two days. Alone, he lay there too weak to move, forgotten in the mass exodus of all living things. He felt the grayness that had enveloped him for so long return. It clouded over him, oppressing his frail attempts to re-ignite the light that, dimmed for so long, was threatening to go out again. It felt easy to give into the gray cloud as it washed over him. He closed his eyes and felt it shroud him once more. It was comforting in its familiarity. He told himself there was no reason to resist the overwhelming sadness. It was, after all, what his life had become used to since the oil spill. He convinced himself that the glimmer of light he had experienced had been a fluke, a temporary moment of brightness in a life otherwise blocked from the sun. The white raven, Zak told himself, had been nothing more than a fantasy of cruel proportion. He felt his eyes roll back underneath their closed lids as his breath nearly ceased to exist. Then, in a surprising surge of uproarious release, he lifted the oppressive weight of his head and body from the ground, extended his neck, and screamed again, louder than even before. He screamed for his soul, for his heart and for his life. Bursting with strength, he flapped around under the tree and screamed with fury for every beat of joy his heart had repressed all these years. Over and over, he screamed until lights began flashing in his head. He screamed for those lost and for those found and mostly he screamed for himself.

When the storm was over and the other ravens found him the next day, Zak's feathers were still partly white from the struggle he had engaged in to reclaim his inner light.

"Thank the great Almighty we found you," his friends cawed as they dipped their wings in a puddle nearby and held them over Zak to let the water drip onto his parched beak.

Zak let the drops fall into his mouth as he gazed gratefully at his friends.

"For a while, there, we thought we lost you forever," one of them said.

The impact left by the storm was far reaching. Although injuries were minimal and no deaths had occurred, damage throughout the Valley was extensive. Businesses, without power for a week or more, were struggling to provide service. Children stayed home from school. Like those who were dealing with the blown off roof of the school and similar damages throughout the area, individuals were trying to tend to damage to their own property.

On the day after the storm ended, the morning newspaper featured a picture of three semi-trucks thrown onto their sides by the tremendous force of a crosswind they had been unlucky enough to drive into. Several buildings that once had metal roofs now looked like giant sardine cans with their roofs either missing or rolled up to their peaks. Traffic signals were non-functional due to massive power outages.

As if the wind had not been bad enough by itself, wind chills of greater than fifty below had caused pipes to burst in homes and businesses all over the Valley. There was debris scattered everywhere the eye could see, and probably even beyond that. The standing water left by the rapid snowmelt only a week earlier *had now frozen into masses of ice all over the area. Polished by the blasting sand of the storm, the ice on the parking lots was especially treacherous, with more than the usual number of fall injury victims reporting to doctors and emergency rooms across the Valley.*

Wild animals, so often seen around the area, were nowhere to be found. It seemed like weeks passed before the first moose strolled through neighborhoods, or maybe it was just that people were too busy to notice if they did.

Doug and Minnie lived in one of the neighborhoods hit hard by the storm. They awoke the first Thursday morning of the storm to find water gushing down their walls and through the floors of their house. A pipe inside the back wall that faced the onslaught of the wind had frozen, and then burst. Unable to reach contractors to deal with the mess, they spent most of the day trying to contain the damage before falling, exhausted, into bed that night. They soon learned that their problem paled in comparison to what many across the region were dealing with. With nothing to do but wait, they drove around the Valley the next morning to survey the damage.

The devastation they saw was overwhelming. Plastic grocery bags hung like ornaments from every branch of every tree as far as the eye could see. Shingles were everywhere except on the roofs of the houses where they belonged. Metal roofs were rolled up like window shades and many buildings with broken out windows all around them had gaping holes in their roofs.

As they drove around, Doug and Minnie could not find one structure that had been untouched by the storm. On one of the main highways through the area, they saw the three semi-trucks that had been blown over by the wind. They were still lying there days after they had been overturned, with no one available to move them off the road.

People could not believe the devastation wrought by the storm. Distressed and amidst staggering amounts of damage, they called for help from contractors who were too overloaded from emergency calls to even respond. Everywhere you looked, the job was immense. With no workers available and people exhausted from living with the damage, the situation looked dire and the forecast bleak.

Zak had flown with his friends back to the Valley to survey the devastation. Still shaken at being caught up in yet another massive natural disaster, he took in the damage all around him. As grateful as he was to have survived, he was even more grateful that he had been able to hang onto his newly re-kindled inner light. As he flew with his friends, Zak re-lived the events of the terrible day the storm began, remembering each moment as if it were happening right now. The thoughts made him tremble. They made his heart race and made him want to fly to some distant place away from the Valley. Instead, he returned to his tree near the glacier and tucked himself into the notch that now served as his home.

It had not been easy to hold onto the glimmer of hope that dwelled within during the storm when he had screamed himself to exhaustion trying to save his raven friends. Lying exhausted under his tree, he had looked out at scores of dead birds and damaged landscape, and felt he was losing all hope or will to survive. Even now, he felt he needed to exert a conscious effort to keep from sliding backwards in despair.

He had come close to giving up that day under his tree. As grateful as he was that the other ravens had found him and not left him alone in this disaster, Zak now realized that it had been he, alone, who had found his own inner strength. In the simple recognition of the goodness in others, Zak had kindled his own inner light. In realizing he could not control the wild forces of nature or the destructive actions wrought by others, he had also learned to forgive himself for things for which he was not to blame.

Zak summoned the courage to come out from under the protection of his tree. In spite of his fears, he joined the other ravens to help begin cleaning the river valley of the carnage of dead birds left by the storm.

"So much for the greatness of the white raven," one of his old buddies from his days in the berry trees chided him as they moved the last dead bird from a gravel bar in the riverbed.

"Didn't stop the disaster, did 'ee, the wondrous white raven?" cawed another.

Zak ignored them; stopping short of giving one of the snappy retorts that he would have indulged in before he met the white raven.

"They just don't understand," one of the friends who had helped with his rescue told him.

"I know," Zak replied. "I'm not the one who can make them see. All I can account for is me. I'm just glad I survived." Strutting around on the ground, he stopped to pick up a stone before idly throwing it down with his beak.

"I can't make much sense of it all, but I can tell you this much," Zak said to his friend, "Even though I will never forget that I was there or what I saw, I find comfort in knowing that as bad as it was, I wasn't a coward."

Zak walked slowly in widening circles on the ground before flying back under the tree that had become his home. His friend followed closely behind. Thinking before he spoke, Zak told his friend, "If there's one thing I learned from what's happened, it's that now I know who I am and what I am made of."

The two ravens drank from the puddle near Zak's tree and rested. In the solitude of the moment, no more words were said. For Zak, his words had not been so much an explanation to his friend as they had been an affirmation for himself.

After a while, the two ravens flew back toward the valley to join the others. On their way past the old trestle bridge, they stopped to gather up hundreds of ravens who had fled there after the storm. Standing atop the bridge, Zak looked down at them. At that moment, it came to him. Who better to take on the immense cleanup of the valley than ravens?

"The people are too burdened to take care of the plastic bags in the trees and shingles on the ground hiding in places only we can see," Zak cawed, feeling the words come from deep within.

"It's up to us to help restore the Valley to the place of beauty that we once enjoyed," he went on, beginning to feel empowered by the responsibility he was undertaking.

Fluttering about on the ground, the ravens listened and pecked their wings in approval.

"This valley is our home, too," Zak cawed, strutting back and forth on top of the old bridge.

Fluffing his hackles and emitting a series of clacks and whistles, he called the birds to action. He spoke to them in Ravenspeak, using their own Valley dialect, as he urged them to join him in his quest to rid the area of the devastation wrought by the storm.

The ravens continued to gather together. With the help of his friend, Zak separated them into groups of twenty birds, each led by a team captain. While they organized, five scouts were dispatched over the Valley. Their job: to designate clean-up regions and locate dumpsters within those regions. When the scouts returned, the plan completed and the teams arranged, the ravens flew off in a massive wave of flapping black resolve. Their speed was amazing. In the course of one day and one night, they removed every plastic bag from every tree and every blown shingle that had been flung to the ground from the Mat-Su Valley floor. All around the Valley, dumpsters were filled to capacity by the efforts of the birds.

At first, people stood dumbfounded by the sight. Then, realizing the help being provided by the ravens, they dispatched trucks to replace the filled dumpsters with empty ones, barely switching full ones with empty ones before they had to do the switch again. Across town, in the area landfill, the pile of debris grew to mountainous proportions as bulldozers worked non-stop to level the incoming trash. Working relentlessly, the birds were too busy to notice the faded red station wagon that slowly followed them around, nor the man who observed them with binoculars as they went about their work.

When they were done, the ravens gathered on the fences around the landfill and slept. As dawn loomed, the snow-capped mountains reflected a growing brightness as one by one scores of ravens began to turn white. Then, just as quickly as it had begun, the birds returned to their natural color until, finally, the transformation was complete. Zak watched them from his perch on a large crane used by the dump. He felt his heart fill with pride as he saw the goodness unfold before him. Even the old sourdough ravens from the berry tree sat on the fences with the others, their own wings tinged in a frosty glow. For the remainder of the month of April, the scene repeated itself until all sections of the Valley were clean of any remaining debris. Not wanting to be the focus of attention for doing only what anyone in such circumstances would do, Zak flew back to his tree. There, he stayed for the next several weeks.

Chapter Nine

Once More, With Feeling

People affected by the devastating spring storm and its aftermath were anxious to put the past several weeks behind them. By early May, most of the repair work around the Matanuska Valley had been completed and the first signs of spring were beginning to emerge. Strawberry shoots were among the first to sprout in home gardens, peeking out from their winter bed of rocky slopes. Horsetail, bluebells, and wild roses appeared in rapid sequence, giving beauty again to the Valley.

The deep potholes and puddling of slushy street ice was now gone, as city crews worked to remove the splay of gravel used for traction control that had accumulated on the roads. Dingy remnants of snowberms remained in a few shaded areas and, although the trees had not yet leafed out, there was now a hint of green in their branches.

Over the next several weeks, large numbers of ravens were seen flying over the area. During this transition of spring, the magpies began to return, followed by robins and then the northern migrations of massive numbers of trumpeter and tundra swans, Canada geese, and sandhill cranes. The moose, so much a part of the landscape during the winter, were now scarce except for the backyard births of sprightly little calves that were making their way into the world with the rest of spring's bounty.

On the lakes the ice was unstable, a soft rotted mess leading to splotches of open water. Atop this seemingly tenuous surface, sat the diehards of ice fishing, perched confidently on the overturned buckets they used for seats. One group of them in particular, talked as they fished, of plans for the annual ceremony to be held at the Veteran's Wall of Honor in Wasilla on the upcoming Memorial Day, now only a few weeks away.

Zak and a few other ravens were among the last winter inhabitants to leave the Valley that spring. After returning to his hollow under the tree near the glacier, Zak had remained rather scarce around his old haunts. Aside from flying out from under his tree for food for his cache, or just to catch a thermal over the river, he stayed away from the mainstream. Life felt somehow better now. Tempered by the struggles he had survived, he enjoyed a new sense of calm. He was thankful he had found this place of peace and all he really asked for was enough serenity to maintain it for each new day.

One of the things that the white raven had told him was, "In order to love yourself, you need to be honest with yourself."

At the time he heard them, the words had not made sense. This time of awareness near the glacier had brought clarity and perspective to those words. For this, he was grateful. After all, Zak now realized, how could he help what had happened over all those years since the oil spill? Up until he had experienced all that devastation, he had been just a normal bird. He hadn't deliberately set out to flail in the pond of life's realities. Instead, he had done what he could, when he could, to survive.

For a time survival had meant burying the images he had seen. For a time, it had left him in the throes of angry retort. Later, survival had meant finding ways to numb the memories from his mind, and for a while it had meant hiding those realizations from himself. Although once convinced that there could be no light in a world that allowed bad things like the oil spill to happen, Zak now knew that he was his own light, and that he alone was responsible for nurturing his own precious inner flame.

It wasn't that Zak had purposely slipped into a state of grayness after the spill. He had tried to talk about what happened with other birds when he came back, but in the best-case scenario, they had called him a whiner and a loser and told him to just get over it. In the worst, there had been total indifference to his plight. Some had even called him a fool for even going to the beaches on that day. Once the terrible oil spill had happened, they asked him, why had he had kept going back to try to help when it had obviously upset him so much to be there? Accused of causing his own pain by going back, they told him that the situation being hopeless then, and now nothing more than history, was best left forgotten. After all, he had been informed, he wouldn't have had to deal with it if he had not chosen to be there.

Eventually, Zak had learned to stay silent about his traumas. Trying his best to return to his normal life after the oil spill, he had quickly learned that normal was a concept that he could no longer grasp. Somewhere along the way he had lost the essence of who he was. And so began Zak's years long descent into the blissful oblivion that only the berry trees seemed to provide. Now all of those years were nothing more than a blur, making him wonder how he could have let the song in his heart stay silent for so long.

Toward the end of May, renewed, Zak left his tree to rejoin the other ravens. It was time. Flying west toward the horizon on the last day of May, the ravens found themselves flying above a large gathering of people near a sprawling, polished piece of granite on the outskirts of Wasilla. To their right were the gently sloping mountains that sheltered Hatcher Pass. To their left, three tall jagged peaks and one flat one that formed the perfect backdrop to the wall upon which were etched countless names of Alaskan veterans. Looking down at the mass of humans gathered in this place, Zak saw William D bundled in his brown army blanket and sitting in a wheelchair near the front of the crowd. Beside him stood Sophie and Donald, with Sophie holding baby Louisa Anne bundled in blankets in her arms.

As the ravens flew over, a uniformed man standing on a garden pathway lifted a bugle to his lips. Some people near him wore military insignia, some were in full uniform as they faced the polished wall of stone, but most were dressed in the ordinary clothes of ordinary people.

"Now, if you will all please stand and face Mt. POW/MIA," a voice boomed over the loudspeaker, "that is the flat mountain behind the wall," the voice continued, "the ceremony will begin."

Lloyd, the flag-keeper, had just finished raising a row of brightly colored flags on the individual flagpoles that lined the bluff behind the wall. They stood with colorful pride against the snow-capped mountains behind. He began to raise the bold stripes and bright stars of the largest flag in the middle of the others just as the bugler finished his refrain. Proudly, he noted how its colors of red, white, and blue snapped sharply in the stiff wind. The flag was almost to the top of the pole when a big gust of wind tore it loose from the rope. People gasped, as the flag fluttered erratically above their reach. Lloyd ran after it, knowing that protocol demanded he catch it before it touched the ground. The brisk wind, however, kept it buoyed overhead, fluttering far beyond his reach. The ceremony was in danger of being ruined.

As the audience stood helplessly in stunned silence, Zak led the other ravens out beyond the edge of the bluff where the flag was now floating away from the crowd. Circling the fluttering cloth of red, white, and blue, the birds gently grabbed the edges of the flag with their beaks and carried it over the silent crowd. Stares of disbelief and tears of joy came to the eyes of many, as the ravens carried the flag within reach of Lloyd, who took it from their beaks. Without ever letting it touch the ground, they held onto the flag as Lloyd re-attached it and hoisted it up the flagpole just as the military jets flew over it in the missing man formation that marked the ceremony every year.

Everyone rose from their chairs and many saluted as the bugler played the National Anthem of the United States of America, thus completing the ceremony. The people in the crowd, many of them veterans of wars come and gone, and others with loved ones in present wars, now saw the actions of these birds as a symbol of the goodness and resilience of their nation.

Some of the ravens had found their white raven in this act. With many of the birds still in transition from white to black, some people thought they saw eagles, while others knew they were ravens.

A native Alaskan, an elder some said, and one of the last veterans of the second Great War said others, summed it up with his softly spoken words to those around him, "The raven is the eagle is the raven. They are such tricksters."

Standing beside him, Wils Kelderman nodded as he pulled out a notepad to document the man's profound words. It had taken him sixty four years, but Wils had finally learned the lesson that had freed his own inner light from the dark cloud that shadowed it for so long, he had learned that listening is the key that opens the heart to understanding.

Turning to the man beside him, Wils nodded knowingly before turning his attention back to the ceremony. All around him, others sat silent, unsure of what to think about the scene they had just witnessed. Someone looked up and pointed as all eyes turned up to the sky. It was then that Wils saw Zak leading the others above the crowd. He knew it was Zak by the wayward tufts of his hackles.

As the raven who had been the focus of his study circled around an old man wrapped in a brown blanket in a wheelchair, Wils Kelderman noted with the accuracy of the historian he was, that the raven Zak tipped his right wing to the old man before leading the other ravens away from the crowd. Wils then sealed the moment in the annals of history by inviting three randomly selected witnesses in the crowd to affix their signatures to his document. Later, he would integrate the manuscript into the archives of his work that chronicled the behavior of ravens.

Flying off into the haze of the oncoming clouds that were now circling in wispy curls around the mountains, the ravens flew toward the peaks beyond. By the time their feathers had returned to their natural color, they had already disappeared from sight.

Later, walking alone on the garden path that held the wall where the ceremony had been, Wils

Kelderman thought about the ravens. Leaning over to pick up a black feather tinged on the edges in white, he began musing about what he had seen. He remembered the way the ravens had come together in flight to save the flag and recalled how some people had mentioned seeing white streaks on some of the birds. Never before had he seen the ravens act in this way, or was it that maybe he just had never noticed before?

Twirling the feather slowly between his thumb and forefinger, he remembered seeing the ravens clean the valley after the terrible storm of a couple of months ago. The white edges of the feather caught the sun as he turned it in his fingers, making it glitter as if covered in frost, but it was too warm now for ice to form. Something made him lay the feather atop the center of the wall that held the names of so many who had served their country with honor. He watched it flicker in the breeze before falling into one of the cracks that joined the sections of the wall into one continuous length. Looking around for the ravens, he saw nothing but magpies where the ravens used to be. The feather flickered once again in the sun before falling to the ground in front of the wall. Wils picked it up and tucked it inside his notebook. Later, he would place it with the document that chronicled this days event.

Above, a caw and a chortle rang out over Wils' head as, startled, he caught a glimpse of the raven Zak again flying away from the wall toward the mountains. Quietly, he took a notepad from his pocket. Pulling out a pen, he noted that on this day he had seen the lone raven, Zak, recognized by the skewed feathers on his throat, return to visit the wall after having earlier been seen flying off toward the mountains.

As quickly as he had appeared, Zak disappeared again and Wils Kelderman saw him no more. Neither did he see any of the other ravens that had peppered the valley all winter. He looked for ravens in the coming weeks, but it was to no avail. Finally, by the middle of June, Wils realized the ravens were not coming back any time soon. Standing in the silence of this place of honor, he made a commitment to himself to undertake a study addressing the question he had heard asked during his studies so often by so many, "Where *do* ravens go in the summer?"